VETERINARIAN

By William David Thomas

Reading Consultant: Susan Nations, M.Ed.,
author/literacy coach/consultant in literacy development

Gareth Stevens
Publishing

Please visit our web site at **www.garethstevens.com.**
For a free catalog describing Gareth Stevens Publishing's list of high-quality books,
call 1-800-542-2595 (USA) or 1-800-387-3178 (Canada).
Gareth Stevens Publishing's fax: 1-877-542-2596

Library of Congress Cataloging-in-Publication Data
Thomas, William David.
    Veterinarian / by William David Thomas.
        p. cm.
    Includes bibliographical references and index.
    ISBN-10: 0-8368-9197-X   ISBN-13: 978-0-8368-9197-3 (lib. bdg.)
    ISBN-10: 0-8368-9330-1   ISBN-13: 978-0-8368-9330-4 (softcover)
    1. Veterinarian—Juvenile literature.   2. Veterinary medicine—Vocational guidance—
Juvenile literature.   I. Title.
    SF56.T84   2008
    636.089—dc22   2008010379

This edition first published in 2009 by
Gareth Stevens Publishing
A Weekly Reader® Company
1 Reader's Digest Rd.
Pleasantville, NY 10570-7000 USA

Copyright © 2009 by Gareth Stevens, Inc.

Senior Managing Editor: Lisa M. Herrington
Creative Director: Lisa Donovan
Designer: Paula Jo Smith
Photo Researcher: Kimberly Babbitt

Picture credits: Cover, title page: © Corbis; p. 5 © Richard Hutchings/Corbis; p. 7 (left)
© Peter Weimann/Animals Animals; p. 7 (right) © Jessie Cohen/National Zoo/Handout/
Reuters/Corbis; p. 8 Photodisc/Getty Images; p. 9 © Richard Hutchings/Corbis; p. 10 ©
David Butow/Corbis; p. 11 © Waltraud Grubitzsch/Corbis; p. 12 © Tom Stewart/Corbis;
p. 13 Shutterstock; pp. 14–15 © Sabina Louise Pierce/University of Pennsylvania/Handout/
Corbis; p. 16 Index Stock/Jupiter Images; pp. 18–19 © Anthony Reynolds/Corbis; pp. 20–21
© Reuters/Corbis; pp. 22–23 © Jessie Cohen/epa/Corbis; pp. 24–25 © Penny Tweedie/
Corbis; pp. 26-27 David Young-Wolff; p. 28 © Erik Freeland/Corbis

Printed in the United States of America

1 2 3 4 5 6 7 8 9 10 09 08

CONTENTS

Words in the glossary appear in **bold** type the first time they are used in the text.

CHAPTER 1

PET PROBLEMS

A **veterinarian** was working at a zoo in England. The veterinarian (or "vet" for short) had a big problem. An animal had arrived from Australia. But it wasn't a kangaroo or a koala. It was a poisonous snake called a death adder. It was sick and needed medicine. But how do you give medicine to a death adder?

The vet got something he knew the snake would eat — a mouse. He gave the mouse a large **injection** of the medicine. Then he put the mouse into the snake's cage. Within minutes, the medicine — and the mouse — were inside the snake. A few days later, the snake was better. Problem solved.

From Legs to Flippers

Veterinarians face problems like this every day. Keeping animals healthy is a tough job. An animal can't tell a vet what is wrong. It's not like treating people. All people have the same kind of heart, lungs, and bones. But animals are not alike. A cat has one stomach, but a cow has seven. A dog's leg is very different from a seal's flipper. Diseases that kill sheep may not bother birds. Medicine that helps a horse might harm a pig. Vets have to know all of this and much, much more.

This Pomeranian puppy's ears look good. Young animals like this should see a vet twice a year.

How to Become a Vet

It takes a long time to become a Doctor of Veterinary Medicine (DVM). First comes four years of college. Veterinary school is four more years. Three years are spent learning about animals, diseases, and medicines. One year is spent working with vets in an animal hospital or a **clinic**.

Some vets go on to become experts in one area. It may be animal cancer, eye treatments, or blood diseases. This takes another two to five years of study.

And vets must continue to learn as long as they work. They take classes and read studies on new medicines and treatments.

Where They Work and What They Do

There are more than 62,000 veterinarians in the United States. Most care for small animals, especially pets. Others care for large animals like cattle, horses, and sheep. Their work is often done in fields or barns.

Vets also do research for companies that make medicines for animals. Pet food makers use vets to help make their products better. The U.S. government hires vets as food inspectors. They help make sure that the meat and poultry we eat are safe and clean. In addition, vets work in zoos, animal parks, and circuses.

Today's Pastime, Tomorrow's Career

If you think you want to be a vet, start working now! Vets say you can start by caring for your own pets. Read about them. Learn their habits. Next, care for other people's pets. Walk your neighbor's dog. Feed your friend's cat when she's away for the weekend. Volunteer to clean cages or feed animals at a pet store, a zoo, or an animal shelter.

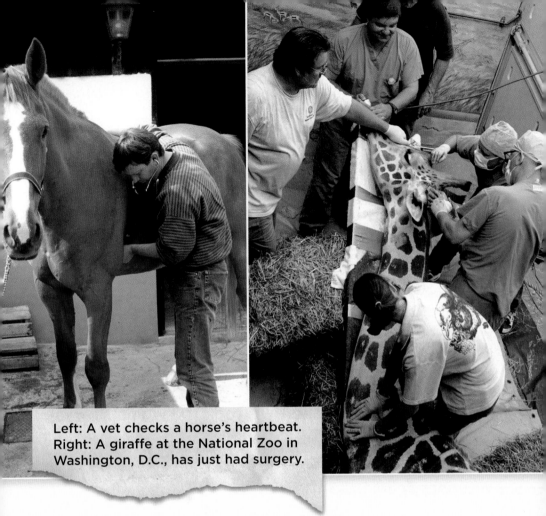

Left: A vet checks a horse's heartbeat.
Right: A giraffe at the National Zoo in
Washington, D.C., has just had surgery.

Could You Be a Veterinarian?

If you're considering a job as a vet, ask yourself these
questions:

- Do you love animals and want to help them?
- Do you like working with people, too?
- Are you interested in science?
- Are you calm and patient?
- Do you pay attention to details and like
  solving problems?

If so, a career as a veterinarian could be for you!

CHAPTER 2

PET VETS

Patti Schroeder took her kitchen sink to the vet. Why? After dinner one night, her husband, Rich, threw fish scraps into the garbage disposal. Rudy, their cat, smelled the fish and jumped into the sink. His head got stuck in the garbage disposal!

Free Rudy!

Rich took apart the disposal. Next, he disconnected the water pipes. He and Patti took the whole sink out of the counter. Rudy stayed stuck. Finally, they put Rudy — and the sink — in the car and drove to a veterinary clinic.

Pets: By the Numbers

Americans have a lot of pets. They own 53 million dogs, 59 million cats, more than 12 million birds, and 7 million other pets. In 2005, Americans spent almost $36 billion caring for those pets.

Open wide! Like people, pets need to have their teeth checked and cleaned.

The vet gave Rudy a shot to make him sleep. He freed Rudy from the sink, but the cat was cold and going into shock. The clinic team covered Rudy with blankets and a hot water bottle to keep him warm. They gave him fluids through an **IV unit**. Rudy stayed in the clinic overnight. The next day he was fine, and Patti brought Rudy home.

Preventive Care

Rudy was cared for by a small animal vet. These men and women treat birds, guinea pigs, lizards, rabbits, and other animals that people keep as pets. Most of their work, of course, is with cats and dogs. A lot of that work is considered preventive care. This means they try to keep pets healthy instead of treating them after they're sick.

Most pets — cats and dogs especially — should have a checkup two times a year. The vet uses a stethoscope to listen to the pet's heart and lungs. The animal is weighed, and its temperature, eyes, and ears are checked. Fur is examined for fleas. Teeth are checked, too. If the animal's teeth need to be cleaned, the vet will give it an **anesthetic** to make it sleep. Dogs and cats won't stay still without it.

Hold still, bunny. A helper holds this rabbit while the vet checks its nose.

The vet may use a needle to take a small sample of blood. The blood is tested to see if the animal has diseases. Dogs are often tested for **heartworms**. Cats are checked for **leukemia**. Pets may get shots protect them against **rabies** and other diseases.

An iguana gets a squirt of medicine.

Emergency Care

Small animal vets do more than checkups, however. Pets get hit by cars. They get hurt in fights with other animals. They get sick suddenly. Some even get

On the Job: Veterinarian

Dr. Douglas Brum works at an animal hospital in Boston, Massachusetts. He directs a wellness program that teaches pet owners preventive care. He says, "If owners are well-educated, we can catch things before they become a problem."

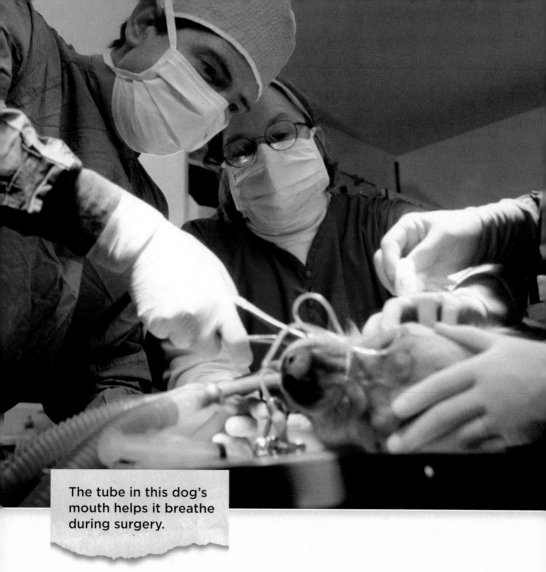

The tube in this dog's mouth helps it breathe during surgery.

stuck in garbage disposals! Vets must deal with these emergencies.

Most clinics or animal hospitals have a special room for taking **X-rays**. These special pictures let the vet see an animal's bones. Another room is used for surgery. Injured animals may have cuts stitched or casts put on broken legs. During surgery, vets wear gloves, masks, and gowns. It's just like surgery in a human hospital.

Death of a Pet

Sometimes animals are too ill or too badly injured to ever get well. When this happens, vets give them medicine. It lets the animal die quickly and without pain. People say the animal has been "put down" or "put to sleep." No vet wants to do this, but sometimes it is best for the animal.

Pet Paperwork

Small animal vets also do a lot of paperwork. They keep records of all their animal patients. They keep track of animals' names, weights, shots, and other treatments. This may be written down or entered into a computer. Vets send out letters to pet owners when it is time for shots or a checkup.

Pet-Care Tips

To take care of your pet, vets say:
- When your pet is young, take it to the vet for shots. **Vaccinations** help keep your pet from getting serious diseases.
- Bring your pet to the vet twice a year for a checkup.
- Don't overfeed your pet. Ask your vet which food is best.
- Make sure your pet gets plenty of exercise and playtime.

CHAPTER 3

LARGE ANIMAL VETS

Barbaro was a big, brown horse with a white spot on his forehead. He sure could run very fast. In 2006, Barbaro won the Kentucky Derby, a famous horse race held each year. A wreath of bright red roses was placed around his neck.

In Memory of Barbaro

Two months later, in another race, Barbaro stumbled. He broke a leg. He was taken to a special animal hospital near Philadelphia, Pennsylvania. The vets placed Barbaro in a giant sling. It held the horse off the ground, so he would not put weight on his broken leg. Despite this, the leg did not heal well. Then Barbaro developed problems with his other legs. Finally, the vets knew the young horse could not get better. Barbaro was put down in January 2007. His owners placed dark roses near his stall.

The cast on Barbaro's leg was not enough to save this famous racehorse. Barbaro won the Kentucky Derby in 2006.

On the Job: Large Animal Vet

Lydia Gray is a large animal vet and the executive director of the Hooved Animal Humane Society in Woodstock, Illinois. Although most of her patients live at the shelter, she has worked in the field, treating horses, cows, and sheep. Gray says the best part of her job is when she saves the life of a sick animal.

No Office Visits

Large animal vets rarely work with pets. They treat working animals, like Barbaro, or animals that are raised for food. The milk we drink and the meat we eat comes from food animals. Large animal vets keep them — and us — healthy.

It's hard to take cows or sheep to a vet's office. Most often, large animal vets go to their patients.

Next patient! This vet will examine a lot of calves today.

They drive to farms and ranches. Their trucks or vans carry the medical tools and medicines they may need. Much of their work is done in barns and fields.

Got Milk?

Many large animal vets work with dairy cattle — cows raised to give milk. Vets treat entire herds. It is very important that dairy cattle are kept clean and free of diseases.

Vets carefully check cows' udders — sacs from which milk is taken. They may take samples of milk to be tested for germs. Vets look at teeth and hooves as well.

Cows cannot give milk until they have a calf. After that, cows must have a calf each year to keep producing milk. Vets are often called to help when calves are being born.

Horses and Hoses

Many people love to ride horses. Horses' hooves and shoes must be checked often. Vets also look at their legs and teeth. Horses often get **parasites**. These may grow in the animal's stomach, blood, or heart. Vets test for parasites. Medicine for parasites is sometimes given through a hose. A vet has to place the hose in the horse's nose.

Large Animal Hospitals

Hospitals for large animals need special equipment. The giant sling that kept Barbaro off his broken leg is one example. Scales for weighing are flat so animals can walk onto them. They're big enough for four feet! Special X-ray machines are designed for use with large animal patients.

Horses, cows, and other large animals sometimes need surgery. Vets use some very high-tech tools. A fiber optic probe is one example. This is a long, thin cable. It has lights, a tiny camera, and small tools at one end. The other end is connected to a computer. Vets use the probe to look inside an animal's body. They can take pictures or collect small samples of skin or bone. With the probe, they may be able to treat the animal without major surgery. And that is safer for everyone.

Vets check this horse's pulse, breathing, and temperature during surgery.

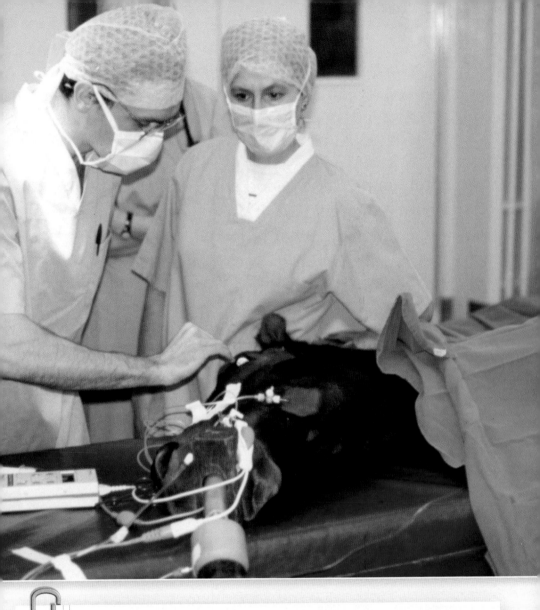

From Horseshoes to Horses

Some of the first vets were metal workers. Blacksmiths made things from metal. One of their biggest jobs was making horseshoes. Because they worked with horses, blacksmiths learned a lot about them. Many blacksmiths learned how to help sick or injured horses.

CHAPTER 4

WILD ANIMAL VETS

Doctor Laurie Gage needed to check her patient's mouth and teeth. But it wasn't easy. For one thing, the patient was swimming. She was a killer whale named Vigga. She weighed five tons (4,536 kilograms) and had teeth as big as your fingers!

No splashing! Dr. Gage uses a waterproof stethoscope to listen to a whale's heart.

Training and Trust

Vigga's trainers worked with her and with Dr. Gage. They had to teach the killer whale to trust them, and to do what they asked. Vigga learned to open her mouth and stick out her tongue so her teeth and gums could be checked. She learned to stay still in the water when Dr. Gage checked her heartbeat. Vigga even stays still when the vet uses a needle to take blood samples.

Captive Animals

Wild animals in **captivity** need special care to stay healthy. Some vets, like Dr. Gage, specialize in helping these animals. They work in zoos, marine parks, and circuses. Disease prevention is most important. Animals must be checked regularly. But many wild animals, such as lions or bears, must be **sedated** first. Only then can a vet take their temperature or check their teeth.

On the Job: Astro-Vet

Martin J. Fettman was the first vet in space. The astronaut-vet flew on the space shuttle *Columbia* in 1993. He did experiments on rats. He learned how the lack of gravity affected their eating, breathing, and walking.

These vets also try to keep their patients active. Animals need exercise, just like people do. Zoo animals, especially, may just lie around in their cages if not encouraged to exercise. Zoo vets create exercise programs and make sure the animals have enough room to move around.

Vets want animals to use their brains, too. Circus animals learn tricks. Zoo animals are given toys. Some elephants are taught to solve puzzles. It's all part of keeping animals healthy.

Endangered Species

Many kinds of animals are in danger of becoming **extinct**. Some wild animal vets work to save these endangered species.

A giant panda cub gets an exam from vets at the National Zoo in Washington, D.C.

- There are very few giant pandas left in the wild. Vets are working with zoos that have pandas. They are helping these animals to have babies. Someday, young pandas may be released into the wild.
- The California condor is a very large bird. They were nearly extinct. Vets worked with others to raise condors in clinics. The baby birds were taught how to find food and live in the wild. Then they were set free. Today, condors are flying in California again.

A Long Run in the Snow

The Iditarod Trail Dog Sled Race takes place in
Alaska every year. The trail is 1,050 miles (1,690
kilometers) long. It takes eight to fourteen days
to finish the race. It's hard on people and dogs.
Thirty-five veterinarians help at the Iditarod. They
check the dogs before, during, and after the race.
Dogs that are injured or too tired are not allowed
to keep racing.

Animals in the Wild

Some vets work with wild animals in the wild. They go into the forests, jungles, or oceans to study animals and protect their health.

For example, wolves once lived in Yellowstone National Park. By the 1970s, they were all gone.

Rangers wanted to bring wolves back. Vets worked with the rangers. They caught wolves in Canada and released them into Yellowstone. Vets kept track of them and their health. Today, wolves are once again roaming the forests in Yellowstone.

Around the world, other vets are working to help and protect wild animals. They are counting elephants in Africa, raising birds in Hawaii, and protecting tigers in India.

On the Job: Veterinary Heart Doctor

Dr. Lynne Nelson is a veterinary cardiologist. That means she is an expert on animal hearts. She found that when a bear hibernates its heart gets weak and the blood gets thick. This is what happens to a diseased human heart. But Nelson says that in spring, "Something makes the [bear's] heart bounce back . . . We hope to apply that to treating diseased human hearts."

A chimpanzee watches closely while a vet checks the eyes of another chimp at a protected animal park in Uganda, Africa.

CHAPTER 5

VET TECHS

Sandy held a stethoscope against the dog's chest and listened. "His heartbeat is strong," she told the vet. "Good," said Dr. Welcher, "I'm nearly finished." The vet was putting stitches in a German shepherd named Fritz. Sandy Sharpe, a **veterinary technician** (or "vet tech" for short), was assisting.

All in a Day's Work

Fritz's owner brought him in the day before. She said the dog had stopped eating. The vet examined Fritz. He asked Sandy to take some X-rays. When the vet looked at them, he found a **tumor**. It had to be removed.

The vet gave Fritz an injection to make him sleep. Fritz's eyes stayed open. Sandy put medicine in them so the dog's eyes would not dry out. Then she shaved the dog's stomach and scrubbed it with **antiseptic**. She got out the instruments the vet would need.

After the operation, Sandy moved Fritz to a cage. She put a large cone-shaped collar on the dog's neck. It would keep him from licking the stitches and pulling them loose. Then Sandy cleaned up the surgical room and tools. It was all part of a day's work for a vet tech.

Talk about wiggly! A vet tech holds this puppy while a vet checks its ears.

So You Want to Be a Vet Tech?

Interested in a workplace filled with a mix of animals that need care and attention? Then consider a career as a vet tech. While most vet techs work in animals hospitals, others work in research labs, zoos, and animal shelters. According to the National Association of Veterinary Technicians in America, vet techs perform the following main duties:

- conduct physical exams and take the patient's history
- teach pet owners how to care for their pets
- care for hospitalized animals
- assist in surgery

- give medicine and vaccines and perform lab procedures, such as checking an animal's blood pressure or taking an animal's X-rays
- perform dental cleanings and exams
- manage animals that are sedated

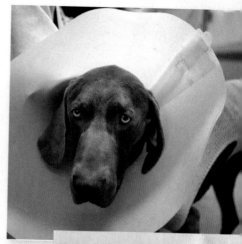

This special collar will keep the dog from licking its stitches after surgery.

Education and Training

Vet techs work with vets much the way nurses work with doctors. All techs need a two-year college degree. Some of them have four-year degrees. Techs usually don't **diagnose** diseases. Most of them cannot write **prescriptions** for medicine. But they do much of the other work needed to care for sick or injured animals to get them healthy again.

On the Job: Vet Tech

Danielle Pratt is a vet tech in Bristol, Connecticut. Part of her job is to hold animals while the vet examines them. Every day is filled with interesting challenges for Danielle. "Animals can't tell you what's wrong," she says. "It's exciting to figure it out."

VETS AND VET TECHS

OUTLOOK

- The United States had about 62,000 veterinarians in 2006. By 2016, there will be about 84,000. The U.S. had about 71,000 veterinary technicians in 2006. Their numbers are growing fast and will reach 100,000 by 2016.

- Most vets are in private practice, in hospitals or their own clinics. Others work for zoos, animal parks, drug companies, pet food makers, and the government. Vet techs work with vets in their offices or clinics.

WHAT YOU'LL DO

- Veterinarians examine animals and diagnose health problems. They give vaccinations to prevent diseases. They stitch and bandage wounds, and perform surgery. Vets choose medicines for animals. They give advice to animal owners on care and feeding.

- Veterinary technicians assist vets. They use X-ray equipment and take blood samples. They schedule checkups, keep records, and help during surgery.

WHAT YOU'LL NEED

- Veterinarians must complete four-years of college. They must then go on to veterinary school for four more years. If they chose to specialize in one type of animal care, they may need two to five more years of study.

- Veterinary technicians must have a two-year degree. Some have four-year degrees.

WHAT YOU'LL EARN

- Vets earn between $47,000 and $133,000 a year.

- Veterinary technicians earn between $22,000 and $33,000 each year.

Source: U.S. Department of Labor, Bureau of Labor Statistics

GLOSSARY

anesthetic — a drug or medicine that causes sleep or loss of feeling

antiseptic — something that kills germs

captivity — being held in one place, such as in a cage or at a zoo

clinic — a place where medical care is given; a small hospital

diagnose — to say what is wrong with an animal after examining it and doing tests

extinct — no longer existing

heartworms — a parasite that lives in the blood or hearts of animals, especially dogs

injection — medicine given through a needle

IV unit — short for intravenous unit; a bag of medicine that drips slowly into veins through a tube and a needle

leukemia — a type of cancer that affects blood

parasites — plants or animals that live in or on another plant or animal

prescriptions — orders for medicine written by a doctor

rabies — a dangerous disease that can be passed from animals to people

sedated — made to feel very drowsy or sleepy

tumor — an unusual growth inside the body

vaccinations — shots of medicine given to prevent certain diseases

veterinarian — a medical professional who cares for the health of animals and treats them for injuries and diseases

veterinary technician — a trained professional who cares for animals and assists a veterinarian

X-rays — pictures taken with special cameras and film that let doctors see the inside parts of a body

TO FIND OUT MORE

Books

A Day in the Life of a Veterinarian. Kids' Career Library (series). Mary Bowman-Kruhm (Rosen Publishing Group, 1999)

ER Vets: Life in an Animal Emergency Room. Donna M. Jackson (Houghton Mifflin, 2005)

I Want to Be a Veterinarian. Stephanie Maze (Harcourt Brace & Company, 1999)

Veterinarian. Exploring Careers (series). Peggy J. Parks (KidHaven Press, 2004)

Web Sites

American Veterinary Medical Association
www.avma.org/care4pets
   Find out more about the path to becoming a vet or vet tech and get animal-care tips, too.

Highlights for Kids
www.highlightskids.com/Science/Stories/SS0798_whalePatient.asp
   Learn more about veterinarian Dr. Laurie Gage and Vigga the killer whale.

The National Zoo in Washington, D.C.
nationalzoo.si.edu/Animals/GiantPandas
   Watch giant pandas on the zoo's "Panda Cam."

The San Diego Zoo
www.sandiegozoo.org/wap/ex_harter_vet_hospital.html
   Take a tour of a veterinary hospital.

INDEX

About the Author

William David Thomas lives in Rochester, New York. Bill has written software documentation, magazine articles, training programs, annual reports, books for children, a few poems, and lots of letters. He claims he was once King of Fiji, but gave up the throne to pursue a career as a relief pitcher. It's not true. This book is for Sandy, a vet tech and a wonderful gift.